# Something Grabbed Me

## Bevis Hanson

Copyright © 2023 by Bevis Hanson

ISBN:   978-1-77883-234-5 (Paperback)

All rights reserved. No part of this publication may be reproduced, distributed, or transmitted in any form or by any means, including photocopying, recording, or other electronic or mechanical methods, without the prior written permission of the publisher, except in the case brief quotations embodied in critical reviews and other noncommercial uses permitted by copyright law.

The views expressed in this book are solely those of the author and do not necessarily reflect the views of the publisher, and the publisher hereby disclaims any responsibility for them.

BookSide Press
877-741-8091
www.booksidepress.com
orders@booksidepress.com

It was dark, the middle of the night, I was all alone in the forest, and it was very, very scary.

Suddenly something moved in the bushes next to me and a hand reached out and grabbed my ankle.

I tried to get away but they were very strong and I was slowly being dragged deeper into the dark forest.

As I was being pulled backwards
I could hear its teeth grinding
and the slurping of its tongue.

"Help!! Help!!" I cried,
"Somebody help me please."

I could feel its hot breath on my face as I closed my eyes and hoped it would eat me quickly so there wouldn't be too much pain.

"Mummy!!! Mummy!!! Where are you" I yelled as my leg disappeared into its foul smelling mouth.

Suddenly I felt somebody pull the thing from the bushes and I heard it yelp as it was spun around and around above my head and then another cry as it was thrown against a tree.

I couldn't believe it, it was my Mum looking so strong and so beautiful and also a bit scary. "Don't you ever touch any of my children" said Mum, "or you will wish you were dead" The creature looked terrified and crept off into the trees whimpering.

Mum took my hand and we walked home together where we ate scones with jam and cream and a nice hot cup of tea. I realised at that moment that my Mum would do anything for me and that I loved her more than anything in the whole world.

www.ingramcontent.com/pod-product-compliance
Lightning Source LLC
LaVergne TN
LVHW071654060526
838200LV00029B/460